GURUJI'S GIFT

written by Alanna Zabel

Illustrated by Mary-Margaret Mitchell

Dedicated to the life and service of
Sri krishna Pattabhi Jois

"yoga is 99% Practice, 1% theory"
∽ Sri k Pattabhi Jois

Published by AZIAM Books

© 2004 Alanna Zabel

ALL rights reserved

www.aziam.com

AZIAM
BOOKS

The PURPOSE of this story
Is about what you give
AnD how your gift will multiply
Depending on how you Live

If you give PureLy from your heart
you will grow enDLess fields of flowers
If you choose not to give
you may never unDerstand these Powers

It was a blazing full moon
Called "Guru Purnima" Day
July, 1915
"Auspicious", some would say

Sri krishna Pattabhi Jois was born
In a small Indian village named kowshika
Three ancient temples made up this village
one to vishnu, Ganapati and shiva

His father was an astrologer
As well as a priest of Hindu faith
He performed many religious ceremonies
Teaching Jois these Vedic ways

one Day at school in Hassan
when Jois was twelve years of age
He watched a Demonstration by krishnamacharya
A wise and well-known sage

krishnamacharya had spent eight years
with his guru in Tibet
studying the yoga sutra's of Patanjali
that he would never forget

Every Day for two years
Jois studied yoga with this man
Practicing breath control, meditation and asanas
until krishnamacharya left Hassan

Jois left home when he was fourteen years old
with two rupees and little more
two friends joined him on their bicycles
they traveled 100 km to Mysore

He Desired to attend Mysore's Sanskrit university
yet having Little money for food he begged
Life was very Difficult for the first two years
until he remembered what his guru had said

"Yoga is not about mastering the postures,"
He said, "but mastering peace of mind"
Jois stopped being angry at his struggles
And instead grew patient and kind

He began offering his love and service
To those who were in need
He picked up trash from the streets
And the hungry he would feed

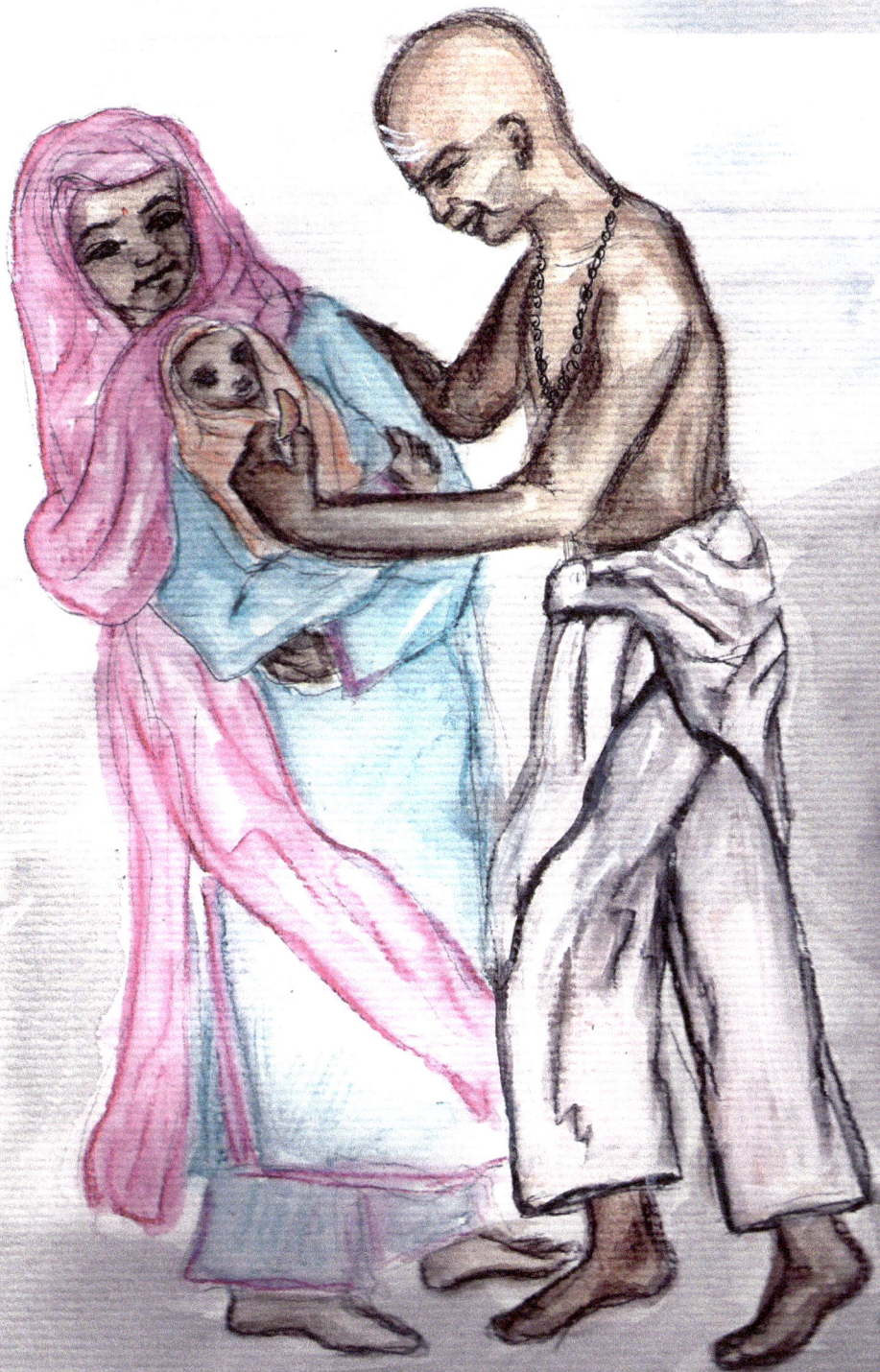

Soon his life was filled with bliss
whatever he needed instantly appeared
He prayed in a temple, asking
"I want to attend Sanskrit university next year"

The next morning he saw a flyer
for a yoga demonstration happening that day
to his delight, it was his teacher and guru
krishnamacharya - horray!

KRISHNAMACHARYA
DEMONSTRATION

Jois walked towards his guru
He prostrated at his feet
Continuing where they left off
krishnamacharya began to teach

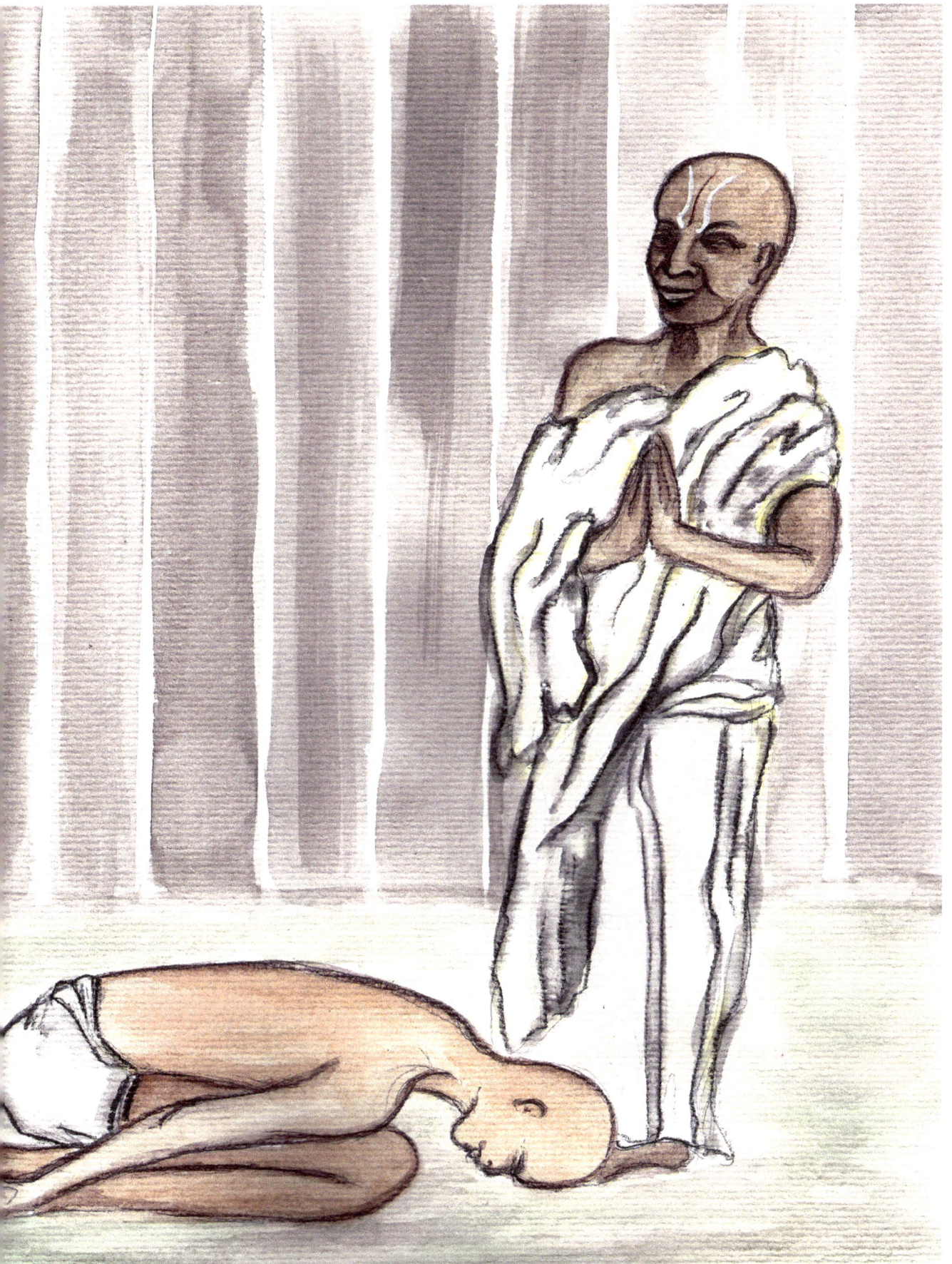

Jois became an advanced teacher of yoga
The royal Maharaja beckoned him to teach
He took kindly to Pattabhi
Inviting him to the university for free

Given a free scholarship
for school, food and pay
In exchange for teaching yoga at the school
Every single day

Jois was so happy and grateful
for his Dream to become real
To teach yoga in exchange for classes
was such an unbelievable Deal!

The Sanskrit University of Mysore

Pattabhi Jois taught yoga for 36 years
At the Sanskrit university in Mysore
Married to his sweetheart, Savitramma
Their love grew more and more

They raised three children
Manju, Ramesh & Saraswati
Saraswati's son, Sharath
would later teach with Pattabhi

He was given the title "GURUJI"
Translating "Dispeller of Darkness"
Teaching millions of people
the Path of enlightenment and bliss

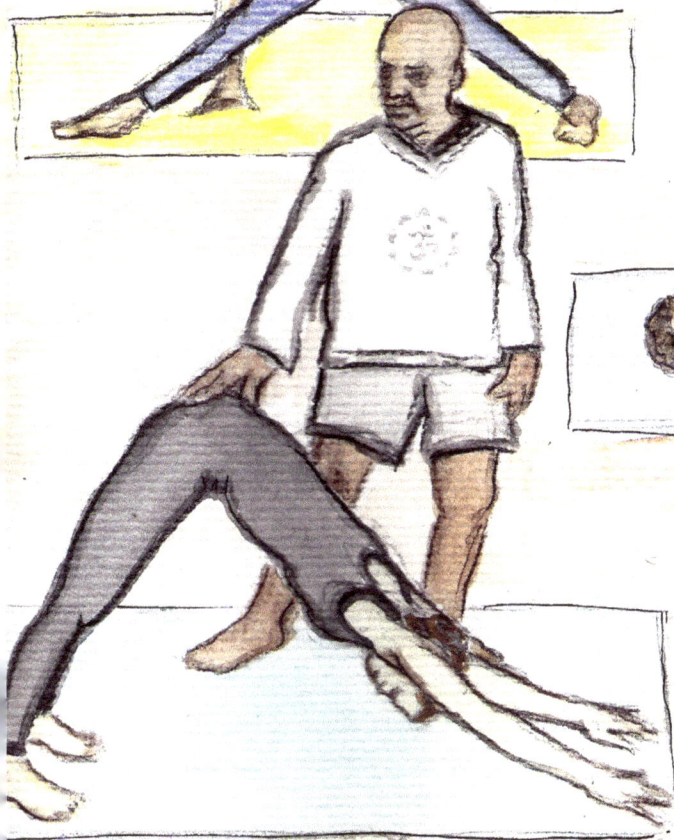

2500 years ago
Patanjali created these yoga teachings
Bramachari, krishnamacharya & Guruji
spread the sutra meanings

these teachings have guided me
And offered great help
If it wasn't for yoga
I'd never have met myself

spread Kindness and Love
To all beings – unknown and known
Together we will restore the world
By giving back. OM.

www.ingramcontent.com/pod-product-compliance
Lightning Source LLC
Chambersburg PA
CBHW040314100426
42811CB00012B/1444